Francis Frith's
LANCASHIRE
LIVING MEMORIES

photographs of the mid twentieth century

Francis Frith's

LANCASHIRE
LIVING MEMORIES

Dennis & Jan Kelsall

FRITH
BOOK Co

08933186

First published in the United Kingdom in 2002 by
Frith Book Company Ltd

Hardback Edition 2002
ISBN 1-85937-335-6

British Library Cataloguing in Publication Data

Francis Frith's Lancashire Living Memories
Dennis & Jan Kelsall

Frith Book Company Ltd
Frith's Barn, Teffont,
Salisbury, Wiltshire SP3 5QP
Tel: +44 (0) 1722 716 376
Email: info@francisfrith.co.uk
www.francisfrith.co.uk

Printed and bound in Great Britain

Front Cover: Blackburn, The Boulevard c1955 B111001

AS WITH ANY HISTORICAL DATABASE THE FRITH ARCHIVE IS CONSTANTLY BEING CORRECTED AND IMPROVED
AND THE PUBLISHERS WOULD WELCOME INFORMATION ON OMISSIONS OR INACCURACIES

contents

Francis Frith: Victorian Pioneer

FRANCIS FRITH, Victorian founder of the world-famous photographic archive, was a complex and multi-talented man. A devout Quaker and a highly successful Victorian businessman, he was both philosophic by nature and pioneering in outlook.

By 1855 Francis Frith had already established a wholesale grocery business in Liverpool, and sold it for the astonishing sum of £200,000, which is the equivalent today of over £15,000,000. Now a multi-millionaire, he was able to indulge his passion for travel. As a child he had pored over travel books written by early explorers, and his fancy and imagination had been stirred by family holidays to the sublime mountain regions of Wales and Scotland. 'What a land of spirit-stirring and enriching scenes and places!' he had written. He was to return to these scenes of grandeur in later years to 'recapture the thousands of vivid and tender memories', but with a different purpose. Now in his thirties, and captivated by the new science of photography, Frith set out on a series of pioneering journeys to the Nile regions that occupied him from 1856 until 1860.

Intrigue and Adventure

He took with him on his travels a specially-designed wicker carriage that acted as both dark-room and sleeping chamber. These far-flung journeys were packed with intrigue and adventure. In his life story, written when he was sixty-three, Frith tells of being held captive by bandits, and of fighting 'an awful midnight battle to the very point of surrender with a deadly pack of hungry, wild dogs'. Sporting flowing Arab costume, Frith arrived at Akaba by camel seventy years before Lawrence, where he encountered 'desert princes and rival sheikhs, blazing with jewel-hilted swords'.

During these extraordinary adventures he was assiduously exploring the desert regions bordering the Nile and patiently recording the antiquities and peoples with his camera. He was the first photographer to venture beyond the sixth cataract. Africa was still the mysterious 'Dark Continent', and Stanley and Livingstone's historic meeting was a decade into the future. The conditions for picture taking confound belief. He laboured for hours in his wicker dark-room in the sweltering heat of the desert, while the volatile chemicals fizzed dangerously in their trays. Often he was forced to work in remote tombs and caves where conditions were cooler. Back in London he exhibited his photographs and was 'rapturously cheered' by members of the Royal Society. His

reputation as a photographer was made overnight. An eminent modern historian has likened their impact on the population of the time to that on our own generation of the first photographs taken on the surface of the moon.

Venture of a Life-Time

Characteristically, Frith quickly spotted the opportunity to create a new business as a specialist publisher of photographs. He lived in an era of immense and sometimes violent change. For the poor in the early part of Victoria's reign work was a drudge and the hours long, and people had precious little free time to enjoy themselves. Most had no transport other than a cart or gig at their disposal, and had not travelled far beyond the boundaries of their own town or village. However,

by the 1870s, the railways had threaded their way across the country, and Bank Holidays and half-day Saturdays had been made obligatory by Act of Parliament. All of a sudden the ordinary working man and his family were able to enjoy days out and see a little more of the world.

With characteristic business acumen, Francis Frith foresaw that these new tourists would enjoy having souvenirs to commemorate their days out. In 1860 he married Mary Ann Rosling and set out with the intention of photographing every city, town and village in Britain. For the next thirty years he travelled the country by train and by pony and trap, producing fine photographs of seaside resorts and beauty spots that were keenly bought by millions of Victorians. These prints were painstakingly pasted into family albums and pored over during the dark nights of winter, rekindling precious memories of summer excursions.

The Rise of Frith & Co

Frith's studio was soon supplying retail shops all over the country. To meet the demand he gathered about him a small team of photographers, and published the work of independent artist-photographers of the calibre of Roger Fenton and Francis Bedford. In order to gain some understanding of the scale of Frith's business one only has to look at the catalogue issued by Frith & Co in 1886: it runs to some 670 pages, listing not only many thousands of views of the British Isles but also many photographs of most European countries, and China, Japan, the USA and Canada – note the sample page shown above from the hand-written *Frith & Co* ledgers detailing pictures taken. By 1890 Frith had created the greatest specialist photographic publishing company in the

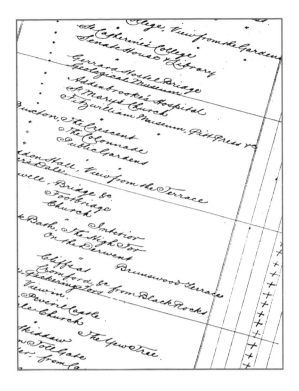

world, with over 2,000 outlets – more than the combined number that Boots and W H Smith have today! The picture on the right shows the *Frith & Co* display board at Ingleton in the Yorkshire Dales. Beautifully constructed with mahogany frame and gilt inserts, it could display up to a dozen local scenes.

Postcard Bonanza

The ever-popular holiday postcard we know today took many years to develop. In 1870 the Post Office issued the first plain cards, with a pre-printed stamp on one face. In 1894 they allowed other publishers' cards to be sent through the mail with an attached adhesive halfpenny stamp. Demand grew rapidly, and in 1895 a new size of postcard was permitted called the court card, but there was little room for illustration. In 1899, a

year after Frith's death, a new card measuring 5.5 x 3.5 inches became the standard format, but it was not until 1902 that the divided back came into being, with address and message on one face and a full-size illustration on the other. *Frith & Co* were in the vanguard of postcard development, and Frith's sons Eustace and Cyril continued their father's monumental task, expanding the number of views offered to the public and recording more and more places in Britain, as the coasts and countryside were opened up to mass travel.

Francis Frith died in 1898 at his villa in Cannes, his great project still growing. The archive he created continued in business for another seventy years. By 1970 it contained over a third of a million pictures of 7,000 cities, towns and villages. The massive photographic record Frith has left to us stands as a living monument to a special and very remarkable man.

Frith's Archive: A Unique Legacy

FRANCIS FRITH'S legacy to us today is of immense significance and value, for the magnificent archive of evocative photographs he created provides a unique record of change in 7,000 cities, towns and villages throughout Britain over a century and more. Frith and his fellow studio photographers revisited locations many times down the years to update their views, compiling for us an enthralling and colourful pageant of British life and character.

We tend to think of Frith's sepia views of Britain as nostalgic, for most of us use them to conjure up memories of places in our own lives with which we have family associations. It often makes us forget that to Francis Frith they were records of daily life as it was actually being lived in the cities, towns and villages of his day. The Victorian age was one of great and often bewildering change for ordinary people, and though the pictures evoke an impression of slower times, life was as busy and hectic as it is today.

We are fortunate that Frith was a photographer of the people, dedicated to recording the minutiae of everyday life. For it is this sheer wealth of visual data, the painstaking chronicle of changes in dress, transport, street layouts, buildings, housing, engineering and landscape that captivates us so much today. His remarkable images offer us a powerful link with the past and with the lives of our ancestors.

Today's Technology

Computers have now made it possible for Frith's many thousands of images to be accessed almost instantly. In the Frith archive today, each photograph is carefully 'digitised' then stored on a CD Rom. Frith archivists can locate a single photograph amongst thousands within seconds. Views can be catalogued and sorted under a variety of categories of place and content to the immediate benefit of researchers.

Inexpensive reference prints can be created for them at the touch of a mouse button, and a wide range of books and other printed materials assembled and published for a wider, more general readership - in the next twelve months over a hundred Frith local history titles will be published! The day-to-day workings of the archive are very different from how they were in Francis Frith's time: imagine the herculean task of sorting through eleven tons of glass negatives as Frith had to do to locate a particular sequence of pictures!

THE FRANCIS FRITH COLLECTION
Photographic publishers since 1860

HOME | PHOTO SEARCH | BOOKS | PORTFOLIO | GALLERY   MY CART
Products | History | Other Collections | Contact us | Help?

your town,
your village

365,000 photographs of 7,000 towns and villages, taken between 1860 & 1970.

The Frith Archive
The Frith Archive is the remarkable legacy of its energetic and visionary founder. Today, the Frith archive is the only nationally important archive of its kind still in private ownership.

The Collection is world-renowned for the extraordinary quality of its images.

The Gallery
This month The Frith Gallery features images from "Frith's Egypt".

the FRITH gallery

News...

Image update complete.
An additional 5,000 images have been added and the quality of all images has now been improved.

Sample Chapters available.
The first selection of sample chapters from the Frith Book Co.'s extensive range is now available. All are offered in Pdf format for easy downloading and viewing.

explore FRITH
Search thousands of photographs from one of the worlds' great archives.

Town search

County search
Select a county

See Frith at www.francisfrith.co.uk

Yet the archive still prides itself on maintaining the same high standards of excellence laid down by Francis Frith, including the painstaking cataloguing and indexing of every view.

It is curious to reflect on how the internet now allows researchers in America and elsewhere greater instant access to the archive than Frith himself ever enjoyed. Many thousands of individual views can be called up on screen within seconds on one of the Frith internet sites, enabling people living continents away to revisit the streets of their ancestral home town, or view places in Britain where they have enjoyed holidays. Many overseas researchers welcome the chance to view special theme selections, such as transport, sports, costume and ancient monuments.

We are certain that Francis Frith would have heartily approved of these modern developments in imaging techniques, for he himself was always working at the very limits of Victorian photographic technology.

The Value of the Archive Today

Because of the benefits brought by the computer, Frith's images are increasingly studied by social historians, by researchers into genealogy and ancestory, by architects, town planners, and by teachers and schoolchildren involved in local history projects.

In addition, the archive offers every one of us an opportunity to examine the places where we and our families have lived and worked down the years. Highly successful in Frith's own era, the archive is now, a century and more on, entering a new phase of popularity.

The Past in Tune with the Future

Historians consider the Francis Frith Collection to be of prime national importance. It is the only archive of its kind remaining in private ownership and has been valued at a million pounds. However, this figure is now rapidly increasing as digital technology enables more and more people around the world to enjoy its benefits.

Francis Frith's archive is now housed in an historic timber barn in the beautiful village of Teffont in Wiltshire. Its founder would not recognize the archive office as it is today. In place of the many thousands of dusty boxes containing glass plate negatives and an all-pervading odour of photographic chemicals, there are now ranks of computer screens. He would be amazed to watch his images travelling round the world at unimaginable speeds through network and internet lines.

The archive's future is both bright and exciting. Francis Frith, with his unshakeable belief in making photographs available to the greatest number of people, would undoubtedly approve of what is being done today with his lifetime's work. His photographs, depicting our shared past, are now bringing pleasure and enlightenment to millions around the world a century and more after his death.

Lancashire Living Memories
An Introduction

DESCRIBED IN A 1930s guidebook to England as one of the richest counties in the land, Lancashire was then, and still is, rightly deserving of such praise. The region's richness extends far beyond the industrial and commercial wealth that the author of the time had in mind, for Lancashire's borders encompass a surprising diversity and interest in its cities, towns, villages and countryside that few other regions rival. True, the south and east can hardly be described as 'pretty', but the towns that were the birthplace of the industrial revolution have other qualities that make them worthy of investigation. The profits generated by their factories and mills were vast, and the investment in civic and commercial building that followed produced some of the 18th and 19th centuries' most eloquent architectural statements. Those same towns were also cradles of cultural development, for in them were established many fine public museums and art galleries, and in Manchester, the German-born musician Sir Charles Hallé founded one of the country's finest orchestras in 1848. In dramatic contrast, Lancashire's wild

countryside can sometimes seem as remote as anywhere: one can roam all day across the moors, hardly meeting another along the way. There are many idyllic corners and attractive villages to be found on the lower slopes and valleys of Lancashire's rolling hills and on the vast coastal plains, huge areas of which were reclaimed from a desolate marshland that once extended along much of its coastline.

For the greater part of its early history though, the region was much less regarded. It took the Romans some 30 years to extend their control over the area from the south. Although they established a number of important forts such as Manchester, Wigan, Ribchester and Lancaster, and created an impressive network of roads, the civilian and agricultural settlements that had grown up elsewhere did not develop, discouraged no doubt by a less favourable terrain and climate and the continuing antagonism of local tribes. Even though the area was later visited by Celtic missionaries from Ireland, and was successively settled by Angles, Saxons and Vikings, by the time William established his

Norman rule over the land, it merited less than a two-page mention in his meticulous and all-encompassing Domesday survey. It was only during the medieval period that the face of the land began significantly to alter with the clearance of large areas of forest; these were replaced by livestock and arable farming.

Over time a thriving woollen industry developed, with fleeces spun and woven in countless scattered farms and cottages and it was the inventive genius of Lancashire men that opened the door to a new era. In 1733, John Kay's flying shuttle' dramatically improved the handloom's efficiency, and in 1764, James Hargreaves invented his 'spinning jenny'. More productive than hand spinning and too big for a small room, it heralded the end of a centuries-old cottage industry. Five years later, Richard Arkwright's 'water frame' first harnessed the abundant waterpower of the fast-flowing Penine streams, and in 1779, Samuel Crompton perfected the technique of spinning fine yarn. Although the mechanisation of weaving took longer to perfect, by the mid 19th-century the whole industry was within the factory system.

The first steam engines were also making their appearance, and soon proved their superiority over water as a power source for the factories. However, without a readily accessible source of coal, the difficulties and costs of transporting the coal limited their economic usefulness. It was Lancashire that again provided the answer, with the country's earliest canals. For the first time, cheap and relatively fast transportation of heavy and bulky goods away from the coast or navigable rivers was possible. The first true canal, the Sankey, was built from St Helens in 1757, with others soon following. The Leeds and Liverpool Canal, which was started in 1770, dramatically changed the face of inland Lancashire, and all manner of industry sprang up along its deliberately sinuous passage through the county. Lancashire also led the way in a second transport revolution, for although the world's first public steam railway had been opened between Stockton and Darlington, Stevenson's pioneering line across the difficult terrain of the waterlogged moss between Liverpool and Manchester marked the real beginnings of the Railway Age. Patterns of life were irrevocably changed, and within a relatively short space of time, there was a mass migration from countryside to town. Cotton had taken the place of wool, and the damp climate of the Pennines proved ideal for the production process. Facilitated by the region's ports and the extensive coalfields around Wigan and St Helens, other industries too were established and expanded, and the area rapidly evolved as one of the major industrial centres of the world.

That same industry was instrumental in the emergence of the numerous holiday resorts that sprang up along Lancashire's coastline. Whilst a few resorts were deliberately planned as genteel places, catering to the needs of a more discerning clientele, the majority set out from the beginning to attract the mass market of the industrial towns, which had suddenly been brought within quick and easy reach by the rapidly-expanding railway network. After long, tiring hours at work in the mills and factories, people wanted pleasure and excitement in their brief holidays. Innumerable hotels and guesthouses were constructed overlooking the coast's expansive sandy beaches, with funfairs, sideshows and theatres being added to provide diversions and entertainment. The development was unconstrained and on a grand scale, with pier after pier striding out to the sea; most spectacular of all was the construction of a 520ft-tall tower at Blackpool, complete with circus, menagerie, dance hall and funfair, all housed within its base. People flocked to the resorts in such numbers that towns had to stagger their recognised holiday weeks to ensure that transport and accommodation could cope with the demand: thus was born the tradition of wakes weeks. The boom continued into the 1960s, when a new concept, the continental package holiday, exploited the resorts' main weakness - the unpredictability of British summer weather. But despite the competition, many of the resorts remain as lively as ever, catering for new markets in day-trips and weekend and winter breaks.

But Lancashire is not all industry and purpose-built resorts, and has much fine, open countryside, often on the very doorstep of the industrial heartland. The Pennine moors and northern hills, whilst perhaps not rivalling the dramatic grandeur of other mountainous areas, have a more subtle beauty, and provide escapes, walks and rambles equal to the best elsewhere in the country. Deep wooded valleys divide expansive rolling moors, from where, on a clear day, there are unbroken views stretching for miles to the Welsh mountains, the Cumbrian fells, and the hills of Yorkshire and Derbyshire. Away from the high ground, there is much gentle, agricultural countryside to enjoy, where one can find attractive villages of stone and brick cottages, still clustered around their ancient church. The Lancashire plains, large areas of which have only been drained from a marshy waste-land since the 18th century, provide some of the most fertile farming land in the country, and market-gardening remains an important

activity. The lush grass supports dairy and cattle farming, and the ubiquitous sheep can be found everywhere from the coast to the highest of Lancashire's hills.

As we wander the county with an inquisitive eye, we will discover countless associations with an interesting and colourful past, for Lancashire has been involved in many of the turbulent events of the island's history. Although far from Scotland, it was not immune from opportunistic bands of border raiders, and it has had a part to play in every civil conflict from the Wars of the Roses to the Jacobite Rebellions. The region has bred its fair share of outstanding people too, who have achieved recognition in just about every field from prime minister to pop star. It was a Lancashire man, Robert Peel, who conceived the modern police force, and it was a Lancashire lass, 'Our Gracie', who helped liven the hearts of a wartime Britain.

Perhaps nothing is more intriguing than the tales surrounding the witches of Pendle, which, despite the centuries that have passed since the documented events occurred, have lost nothing of their power to excite the imagination. The early 17th century was a period of religious persecution and superstition, and paranoia ran high, particularly in Lancashire, which has always been a traditional stronghold of the Catholic faith. Ignorance and prejudice left people all too ready to attribute misfortune or unexplained events to witchcraft, and those who did not readily fit into a community were easy targets for accusation. Under the shadow of Pendle Hill lived two feuding peasant families, the Chattoxs and the Demdikes, each headed by old crones who were both feared and hated by the neighbouring villagers. They were credited with evil powers, and when the Demdikes were charged with theft by their rivals, accusations and counter-accusations of witchcraft and devilry quickly followed. Three of the women were eventually sent to Lancaster for trial, but in a foiled plan to murder the gaoler and free them, others were implicated, including Alice Nutter, a local landowner. In the end, some twenty people were condemned, many admitting their guilt to avoid a torturous inquisition, and were subsequently executed at Lancaster Castle. But the ghosts linger, and to this day, people tell of strange sights and unnatural sensations experienced in the lonely gullies which cleave the steep buttresses of that desolate hill.

The photographs included within this selection show Lancashire as it was in the 1950s and 60s, a time when there was great optimism and prosperity after the hardships of the war years. It was a period of much rebuilding in the towns and cities, firstly to address housing shortages and repair wartime damage, and then to replace the Victorian slums that had been thrown up a century earlier to house the workers flooding from the fields to the new factories.

There was high employment, so people had money to spend on more than the bare necessities of life; and with an increasing number of cars appearing on the road, the first motorways were built. The county's boundaries were different to those of today. They included areas that are still regarded by many people as an integral part of Lancashire: the land of Furness in the far north, which has since been annexed within Cumbria, and the industrial conurbations of the south and east, that were separated as administrative regions in their own right. Since these areas were part of Lancashire when these photographs were taken, and made important contributions to its history, they have been included here.

Although barely 50 years have elapsed since the earliest photographs in this collection were taken, many reflect the numerous and often massive changes that have taken place since then. It is surprising how quickly we can forget 'what was there before they built the new...?' - let us hope that these captured moments in time will jog a few pleasant memories.

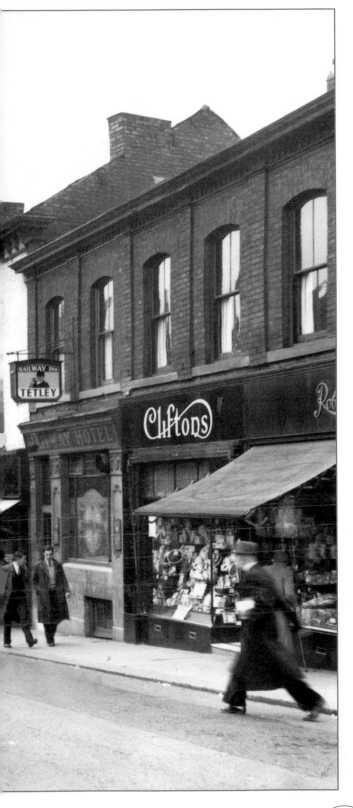

The Industrial South and East

Eccles, Church Street c1960 E88010
Eccles cakes were once made at Bradburns in Church Street. The shop premises by the Railway Hotel were built near the site of a 19th-century graveyard, which was opened to take victims of a cholera epidemic that spread through the town. St Mary's Church, the oldest building in Eccles, stands back from the road, part way along on the left.

▼ Eccles, The Town Hall and Church Street c1960 E88015

Reflecting the prosperity of the Victorian era, the Town Hall was built in 1880 on the site of a cock pit and was later extended to include a police court. The building next door is the Duke of York, and beyond that is the town's main post office. At the far end of the row stands the Broadway Cinema.

▼ Manchester, Market Street and Piccadilly Junction c1965 M21046

Overlooked by the then newly-built Plaza Hotel, Piccadilly Square is a main focus in the city and incorporates a bus terminal and garden area. Lewis's developed during the late 19th century, and at one time was the largest departmental store outside London. Paulden's store opened in the 1950s; the building had been constructed in 1932 as a warehouse.

▲ Bury, The Rock c1955
B257022

Imposing 19th-century buildings line one of Bury's main streets, which leads from the town's parish church, St Mary's. The attractive building on the left was erected in 1874 as the Union Club. Beyond lie Woolworth's and the distinctively-styled Burton's building. By the church stands a statue of Robert Peel, notable because his waistcoat is buttoned the wrong way.

◀ Bury, Kay Gardens c1955
B257011

The gardens commemorate John Kay, born in Bury in 1704 and inventor of the flying shuttle. Mobs ransacked his home fearing that the machine would rob them of work, and mill owners refused to pay his royalties; he ended his days a pauper in France. The copper-domed building behind is the Market Hall, and the Royal Cinema stands beyond.

Rochdale, The Town Centre c1955 R42006
Rochdale is famous as the home of Gracie Fields; its civic centre reflects the booming industrial wealth of the 19th century. Laid out beneath Sparrow Hill, on which stands the 13th-century church of St Chad, is the elegantly spacious Esplanade. It is lined by some of the town's finest architectural heritage, notably the Town Hall, which opened in 1871.

◄ **Liverpool
The Entrance to the
Mersey Tunnel c1955**
L60002
When opened by King
George V in July 1934, the
tunnel between Liverpool
and Birkenhead was the
largest ever built. Two miles
long, 44 feet wide and
dropping 170 feet below
the river, it enabled two
lanes of traffic to travel in
each direction. The first
tolls were dependant upon
horsepower and varied
between one and two
shillings for cars.

Rochdale, The Roman Catholic Church c1960
R42003
Facing the railway station is this unusual Catholic church, dedicated to St John the Baptist. Completed in 1925, its most striking external feature, the central dome, is said to be a quarter of a mile in circumference. Inside, the sanctuary contains a magnificent mosaic depicting Christ the King and John the Baptist.

Liverpool, The Royal Liver Buildings c1955 ▷ L60019
Opened on 19 July 1911 to house the Royal Liver Insurance Company, this was the country's first building to be constructed from reinforced concrete. The famous Liver birds, which gave the city its name, look out across the Pier Head from clock towers 295 feet tall, whose faces are each 25 feet in diameter and larger than those of Big Ben.

▼ Liverpool, The Mersey Ferry c1955 L60021
At one time there were, ferries to New Brighton, Egremont, Seacombe, Birkenhead, Rock Ferry and Eastham, and before the tunnel opened, vehicle ferries also ran to Seacombe and Birkenhead. The Mersey's plucky little boats saw action in both World Wars, and the original 'Iris' and 'Daffodil' were awarded their title 'Royal' for their gallant service at Zeebrugge in 1918.

◄ **Warrington**
The Manchester Ship
Canal c1955 W29010
The idea for a canal into
Manchester was first
conceived in 1697, but
it was 1824 before the
plan was taken seriously.
Work began in 1885,
and sixteen thousand
navvies were employed
in digging the cut.
Queen Victoria opened
the canal in 1894,
which, at its peak in the
late 1950s, annually
carried some 18 million
tons.

◀ Widnes, The Bridge c1960

W97017

Beside the railway viaduct is the suspension road bridge, which opened in 1961. Behind it, constructed in 1905, is the transporter bridge: vehicles and passengers crossed on a suspended platform which was dragged back and forth above the river. It was immortalised in Stanley Holloway's narration of Marriott Edgar's 1933 monologue poem, 'The Runcorn Ferry' ('tuppence per person per trip').

▼ St Helens, Church Street

c1965 S415005

Once upon a time, quiet, low-pollution trolley buses brought people into Church Street, which, before its uninspired redevelopment, was the main shopping thoroughfare. Major high street names stood beside local businesses, and at the far end was the Capitol Cinema, one of several in St Helens. Part way along on the right was the Fleece, the town's main hotel for over 200 years.

◀ St Helens The Town Hall c1955

S415003

The Town Hall opened in 1876, replacing an earlier building that had been destroyed by fire in 1871. It almost suffered the fate of its predecessor when, during redecoration for a visit by King George V, fire again broke out in the tower. Fortunately, a brave painter managed to scale the building with a fire hose and saved the day.

◄ **Adlington, Chorley Road c1955** A338014
Situated below Winter Hill on Rivington Moor, Adlington developed as a textile town before the advent of the railway because of its proximity to the Leeds and Liverpool Canal, which runs behind the main street. Many of its stone cottages were built to house the mill's workers, which still stands on the edge of the town.

Wigan, Market Place c1955

W98004

Despite redevelopment, the facades of these buildings, which cluster around the medieval market place, remain recognisable today. Standishgate's mock-Tudor embellishments were added during the 1920s; with the distinctive Burton's building, they lend elegance to the main shopping street. Associated with George Formby and George Orwell, Wigan was also the butt of music-hall jokes, but the pier does exist.

Rivington, The Road to Rivington Pike c1960

C537009

This strange building, standing on the edge of the moor above Rivington village, is a pigeon tower and summerhouse. It was erected in 1910 for Lord Leverhulme, the son of a Bolton grocer, whose fortune came from the manufacture of Sunlight Soap. He bought the estate in 1899 and later donated much of it to Bolton Corporation.

Adlington, Market Place c1955 A338009

On the corner of Park Road, which leads to the canal, stands a Co-operative shop. These shops achieved success by selling provisions and household goods, many under their own brand name, at value-for-money prices, with the added bonus of a dividend at the end of the year, when the profits were shared amongst its members, the regular shoppers.

▼ Euxton, Wigan Road c1955 E207001

This view looks south along Wigan Road to the Anderton Arms, now managed as an Italian restaurant. During the 17th century, one of the country's first paper mills was built in the village, a far cry from Euxton's industrial role in the 20th century, when a munitions factory began production here shortly before the start of the Second World War.

▼ Euxton, The M6 Motorway from Runshaw Lane c1965 E207014

December 1958 saw the country's first motorway, the M6 Preston bypass. Other sections soon followed, with the Lancaster bypass opening in 1960 and the Thelwall Viaduct, which takes the road high above the River Mersey and the Manchester Ship Canal, being completed in 1965. It was not until 1970, however, that the M6 reached England's northern border at Carlisle.

▲ Withnell Fold
The Cricket Field c1955

W412005

Withnell Fold's Sports and Social Club is still going strong, with facilities for tennis, hockey and bowls, as well as cricket. The tiny hamlet grew around a paper mill, opened in the 1840s by the Parke family beside the Leeds and Liverpool Canal. Its speciality was a high quality paper, used in the production of bank notes.

◀ **Darwen, Market Street**
c1955 D8011

Sharing its name with the river in whose valley it lies, Darwen grew rapidly as a result of industrialisation in the early 19th century, and many of the buildings along Market Street were constructed during that era. At one time, trams ran through the town and the course of the track-bed is still evident along the centre of the street.

Darwen, India Mill Chimney c1955 D8036 ▶
In the 19th century, India was one of the British cotton industry's main customers, and Ghandi himself visited Darwen in 1931. The 303ft-tall chimney of the India Mill must be one of the most elaborate ever designed: completed in 1868, it was 14 years in the making, and is constructed from hand-made bricks.

▼ **Haslingden The Town Centre c1955** H456010
Overlooking the corner of Manchester Road and Deardengate in the centre of Haslingden, and readily identified by the large clock projecting into the street, is the Commercial Hotel. In 1907, Emily Pankhurst addressed a crowd from one of its upper windows, rallying support in her crusade to achieve suffrage for women.

▲ **Blackburn The Industrial Area c1955** B111004
Seen from a viewpoint at the northern edge of Blackburn, above Corporation Park, the forest of chimneys rising above the city is a reminder of the vast number of mills that once operated here. One of them, the Imperial Mill, which began production in 1904, was amongst the largest spinning mills in the world and boasted 100,000 spindles.

◀ **Blackburn
The Garden
of Remembrance c1955**
B111008
In complete contrast is this peaceful scene in the city's Garden of Remembrance, which lies at the southern entrance to Corporation Park. Spread over some 18 hectares, the park was opened in 1857 and was lavishly laid out with flower beds, shrubberies and ornamental lawns. It also contained bowling greens and tennis courts for those pursuing more active recreation.

Blackburn
The Boulevard c1955
B111001
The central bus terminus on the Boulevard stands outside the railway station, from where this photograph was taken. Opposite is the Adelphi Hotel, built at a time when most visitors staying in the city would have arrived by rail. Overlooking the square is a statue of Gladstone, and behind him lie the cathedral grounds.

▼ **Helmshore, Musbury Tor c1955** H63025

Once quarried for its stone, Musbury Tor is typical of Rossendale's countryside, where steep slopes climb from the valley to culminate in an undulating plateau that offers fine walking and grand views. The tall chimney rises from Park Mill, whose mules still operated in the early 1980s. Buildings in the foreground now house the fascinating Helmshore Textile Museum.

▼ **Accrington, The Town Hall c1965** A19025

Erected in 1858 as a memorial to Robert Peel, the Town Hall, whose porch and balcony project into the street, originally served as the Mechanics' Institute until the town was incorporated as a borough in 1878. Behind it stands the Market Hall, which was built in 1869, its façade embellished with reliefs depicting bountiful plenty.

▲ **Accrington Blackburn Road c1965**
A19022
We are looking across the Market Place. The Market Hall is just visible on the left, and the area beside it still serves as the town's main bus terminal. Beside the imposing 19th-century bank building, which overlooks the corner of Blackburn Road, rises a naked steel tower, a herald of the monotonous shopping developments that have robbed character from Britain's towns.

◀ **Bacup, The Fountain St James' Square c1955**
B588035
Many of the town's buildings were constructed during the industrial boom years of the 19th century, including the Mechanics' Hall, now the library, on the left and the Conservative Club, just beyond. The 'Bacup Nats', a local naturalist group founded in 1878, had their home in Yorkshire Street, which lies off the roundabout to the left.

◀ **Nelson, Manchester Road c1955** N146035 Although previously a focus for a cottage weaving industry in the area, the town only developed during the 19th century after the construction of the Leeds and Liverpool Canal. The lofty tower and spire we can see in the distance rises above the now redundant St Mary's Church, which contained two windows by the Victorian Pre-Raphaelite artist, Burne-Jones.

◄ Bacup, St James' Street c1955 B588030

The ornamental floral beds that here border St James' Street have now been removed, but buses still use the area as their terminus. The River Irwell, beside which Bacup lies, powered the first mills in the town, and the Irwell Mill, whose square tower rises at the back, was one of several providing employment in the town.

▼ Nelson, Scotland Road and Leeds Road c1955 N146049

Standing in the centre of the town at the junction of roads to Yorkshire and the north is the extravagantly ornate Union Bank Building, occupied by Barclays in the 1950s and now by the Abbey National. The town's best known pub, the Lord Nelson Inn, lies just off the photograph to the left.

◄ Colne, Albert Road c1955 C600047

Beside the memorial to the dead of two world wars is a statue to another of Colne's brave sons, Wallace Hartley. Appointed bandmaster on the 'Titanic', he kept his band playing as the ship sank, helping to bring calm to the desperate scene. The large cupola adorns the Co-operative building and beyond, the clock tower identifies the Town Hall.

Burnley, Manchester Road c1950 B251026
Burnley was granted a charter in the 13th century; its prosperity grew first from wool and later from coal mining and cotton production. A massive expansion took place with the completion of the Leeds and Liverpool Canal at the beginning of the 19th century, and for a time the town was the world's largest producer of cloth.

Burnley
Manchester Road c1950 B251023
On the left is the Old Red Lion, and beyond stands the Savoy
Cinema and Café. The cupola on the right marks the Town
Hall, and before it, the Mechanics' Institute, which opened in
1855 and remains Burnley's cultural centre. The Dutton's
house got its name 'The Big Window' from being the town's
first pub to have a plate glass window.

The West Lancashire Plain and its Coast

Burscough Bridge
Liverpool Road North c1960 C597005
This view looks along the main road between Liverpool and Preston towards the
railway bridge. The town grew to importance during the latter part of the 18th
century with the construction of the Leeds and Liverpool and Rufford Canals,
which meet by the town. Warehouses sprang up along the quaysides and
boat-building became an important local industry.

▼ Ormskirk, Victoria Gardens c1965 O22090

Granted a charter in 1286, Ormskirk was an important market and industrial centre. Later, brought within easy travelling distance of Liverpool by the railway, wealthy businessmen built comfortable houses away from the city's grime. The park was an essential element of Victorian town development, and here is centred on a memorial to those killed in the South African wars.

▼ Ormskirk, The Clock Tower c1960 O22074

Standing at the cross-roads in the centre of the town is the clock tower, which was erected by public subscription in 1876. It marks the site of the old market cross, and contains a bell dating from 1684 that once served as the town's fire alarm.

▲ Aughton, Town Green c1950 A350008

Stone sets pave Town Green, as it leads through the village towards the railway bridge and station. The Railway Hotel on the left has now changed its name to the Cockbeck Tavern, and Sidney Huyton's general store continues in business, having expanded into the adjacent premises.

◀ **Lydiate, The Mersey Motorboat Club c1955**

L475012

Once the freight arteries of Britain, the canals declined as railways developed. Some were filled in, but others survived to become an important recreational facility. The Mersey Motorboat Club, founded beside the Leeds and Liverpool Canal in 1932, must be one of the first such organisations established, and its clubhouse and moorings still line the waterfront.

Formby
The Post Office c1955 F106003
Formby was once a fishing village, but a retreating shoreline has
left it a mile inland behind an extensive dune system, part of
which the National Trust manages as a nature and red squirrel
reserve. The town grew as a dormitory for nearby Liverpool, and
the neatly-laid-out village centre by the post office and bank is
typical of its planned development.

Southport
The Casino and the Pier c1960 S160174
Once known as South Hawes, the town took its name from the South Port Hotel, which was built in 1790. The pier, opened in 1860, runs over two-thirds of a mile across the marine boating lake and out to sea. Regimented deck-chairs occupy a sheltered spot below the promenade, and in the distance a big dipper marks the resort's funfair.

Southport, Lord Street c1960 S160126
Laid out as an extravagant boulevard in the 1820s, Lord Street's many elegant buildings reflect the town's ambitions as a high-class residence and resort. Perhaps the street's most distinctive feature is the elaborate arcade of decorative cast iron and glass, which projects from the shops for much of its length.

▼ Banks, Hoole Lane c1955 B740002

Along the street on the left stand St Stephen's Institute and the village school; beyond, on Ralph's Wife's Lane, is the church of St Stephen in the Banks. Ralph was a fisherman who failed to return after a violent storm at sea. In despair, his wife spent the night in a fruitless search amongst the marshes for him.

▼ Banks, The Riverside Caravan Holiday Centre c1960 B740017

The booming 1960s economy gave people not only more money but time in which to spend it, and caravan holidays became increasingly popular. The Riverside, which opened in May 1960, was one of many holiday parks established during that era, providing both a place to stay and facilities and amusements to create a complete holiday atmosphere.

▲ Banks, The Clubroom the Riverside Caravan Holiday Centre c1960
B740024

Amongst the attractions on offer was nightly entertainment in the camp's licensed clubhouse. Tables and chairs line the dance floor and spotlights highlight the stage, from which a resident band would provide music. The evening's show often included a comedian and singer, and no doubt half an hour would be set aside for the ever-popular bingo.

◀ Tarleton, Church Road c1955 T199001
Overlooking the main road through the village is the church of the Holy Trinity. It was built in the 1880s to replace an earlier church dedicated to St Mary. Beyond the primary school is the Tarleton Hotel, which has stood in the village since the 17th century and now goes by the name of the Cock and Bottle.

Croston, Church Street c1955 C474008
Tradition holds that St Aidan erected a cross here in 651, and that it is from this that the village takes its name.
The base of a 17th-century cross is partly obscured by the village pump, which stands by a low building that was
once a smithy. At the end of the street stands the 16th-century church of St Michael and All Angels.

Croston, Town Bridge c1955 C474009
Although bearing a date of 1682, this packhorse bridge across the River Yarrow was constructed in 1671. High
walls enclose the water channel, for although the village lies some seven miles from the coast, it is barely above
sea-level: the houses lining the river bank have been flooded many times over the centuries.

Around Preston and the Ribble's Tributaries

Preston
Market Place c1955 P113015
The county's administrative centre since 1798, Preston has long thrived on trade and industry. Amongst its famous sons is Richard Arkwright, who invented the spinning frame. Behind the open-air market rises the cenotaph, designed by Sir Giles Gilbert Scott. Hidden by the trees is the Town Hall, with the Harris Museum standing just out of picture to the right.

Preston, The Market c1960 P113075
This vast open Market Hall was constructed in 1875, and the roof, carried on elaborately decorated cast-iron pillars and supports, covers an area of some 3,500 square yards. It stands at the centre of the town beside the Town Hall, which, although only completed in 1933, embodies the grand architectural style of its neighbouring buildings.

Preston, The Docks, North Side c1960 P113050
Preston docks were once some of the busiest in the country, handling cargoes from around the world. Behind rises the 303-foot spire of the Roman Catholic St Walburghe's Church, which was completed in 1866 to a design by Joseph Hansom, inventor of the Hansom cab. The square tower to its left is the neighbouring Anglican church of St Mary.

Preston
The Tram Bridge c1955 P113007
Although the Lancaster Canal was intended to run from Kendal to
Wigan, the aqueduct planned to take it over the Ribble was never
built. The two halves of the canal were instead linked by a tramway
in 1803, which crossed the river on this bridge. However, multiple
cargo handling proved too costly and the line closed in 1857.

▼ **Bamber Bridge, Stag Lodge c1955** B739007
Stag Lodge is one of the entrances to the grounds surrounding Cuerden Hall.
Several local families have held the estate, including the Towneleys who built the
present hall and an ornamental lake. The Sue Ryder Foundation currently owns
the hall. Despite the forbidding notice on the gate, much of the parkland is now
incorporated within a delightful country park.

▼ **Broughton, The Fire Brigade Headquarters c1965** B718006
Now Fire Headquarters, Hazel Mere was built in 1892 as a family home for
Joseph Foster, a Preston machine maker. Requisitioned by the National Fire
Service during WWII, it was eventually bought for the Lancashire Brigade in 1949.
The extension was added in 1959, with further additions since, but the character
of the building remains substantially the same.

▲ **Lea
Blackpool Road c1955**
L472006
Before the M55
motorway opened,
Blackpool Road, which
passes through Lea on
the outskirts of Preston,
was busy with traffic to
and from the holiday
resort. The Pig and
Whistle, now called
Quinneys, was a popular
stopping place along the
route and needed its
large car park to
accommodate the many
vehicles that pulled in.

◄ **Freckleton**
The War Memorial c1960
F19/023
The gardener is busy at work in this small garden beside the main road in the middle of the village, which contains a memorial to those of the village who lost their lives in two world wars. Nearby another monument remembers two teachers and 38 children, killed in 1944 when an American Liberator from Wharton crashed on the school.

Longridge, Market Place c1955 L340006

At one time surrounded by inns, the square was the site of the old market place and later of a bus terminus. The Dog Inn was built in 1913, replacing a much earlier pub of the same name. The shop to its right was also once a hotel, Swarbrick's Arms, and ahead along King Street were the Red Lion and the White Bull.

Longridge, Berry Lane c1955 L340004

Running from the Market Place to the station and level crossing at the bottom of the hill, Berry Lane leads to today's town centre. The turrets, beyond the barber's shop, decorate the United Reformed Christ Church, which was built in 1865. The tall chimney rises above Crampoaks Mill, and was demolished around 1960.

Longridge
Little Lane c1955 L340014
The town expanded rapidly during the industrial period, and many
of its stone terraces were built to accommodate workers in the
mills. The area was also noted for its quarries in the surrounding
hills, and the high quality stone was used for many grand projects
including Liverpool's docks and several of Preston's civic buildings.

◄ **Chipping, Talbot Street c1955** C598026
At the top of the street is the Sun Inn where, in 1835, Lizzy Dean was a barmaid. Whilst dressing for her wedding, she heard the church-bells ringing; through her window, she saw her betrothed already married to another. Grief-stricken, she hanged herself and was buried beneath the church path, requiring her faithless lover to pass her grave each Sunday.

◀ Chipping, Talbot Street c1955 C598022

Sheep fleeces were the raw material for the five mills which were once working in the village. Chair-making was another speciality, and there is still a chair-maker here by the church. Many of the stone cottages date from the 17th century, and at number 22 lived a cloth merchant, John Brabyn, who founded a Bluecoat school and almshouses in Chipping.

▼ Ribchester The White Bull Hotel c1955 R29015

The Romans established a fort here, Bremetennacum, in AD80 by a ford across the Ribble, and the pillars supporting the porch of the White Bull Hotel are said to have come from one of its temples. The inn was built in 1707 and behind is the site of a 2nd-century bathhouse. Note the mounting block by the entrance.

◀ Ribchester The Almshouses c1960 R29020

These attractive almshouses on Stydd Lane, complete with a well for their water, were built by John Shireburn in 1728 to house five Catholic spinsters or widows. To the left is the Catholic church of St Peter and St Paul, which was erected in 1789, and just along the lane is an older chapel, dedicated to St Saviour.

◄ Hurst Green
Avenue Road c1955

H445003
Beside the drive leading
to Stonyhurst park
stands the Bayley Arms
Hotel, whose name is a
reminder of the original
holder of the manor,
Otto de Bailey. The
family name changed
after his descendant,
Richard, married
Margaret Sherburne,
when their son, also
Richard, adopted his
mother's name.

◄ Hurst Green
The Shireburn Arms Hotel
c1960 H445026

Beyond the war memorial is the Shireburn Arms, whose title comes from the one-time lords of the manor and which carries on its wall their family crest. Hugh Shireburn began the hall at Stonyhurst in about 1523, and his descendant, Nicholas, built almshouses in 1706 at Kemple End. In 1946 they were dismantled and re-sited here at Hurst Green.

▼ Stonyhurst, Woodfields
and the Post Office c1955
S208011

The cottage, built in 1824, served as the local post office; like the rest of the small hamlet, it is part of the Stonyhurst estate. Jesuit monks arrived from Normandy in 1794 and founded a college in the hall. Amongst its pupils have been Sir Arthur Conan Doyle and Charles Laughton, and the poet Gerard Manley Hopkins taught there.

◄ Langho, Whalley Road
c1955 L200011

The original village, Old Langho, lies a mile to the north; the new village grew here alongside the main road after the opening of Spring Mill, whose chimney rises in the background. Weavers, who had previously operated handlooms in their own cottages, came to work the mill's power-looms.

Whalley, King Street c1955 W77031
Park Villas line the main road - they were built at the end of the 19th century and stand near the ruins of Whalley Abbey, whose last abbot, John Paslew, led his monks on the Pilgrimage of Grace in 1536. The protest against the suppression of the monasteries failed, and he and many others were put to death for their objection.

Whalley, The Viaduct c1965 W77061
Whalley's viaduct is the longest in Britain, its 49 arches carrying the railway high above the River Calder. It was completed in the early 1850s, and the countless bricks from which it is constructed were made on the site. Passengers who continue their journey north via Settle enjoy a second treat as they cross the famous Ribblehead Viaduct.

Clitheroe
Castle Street c1950 C122006
Clitheroe is the county's second oldest borough - its
charter was given in 1147. A busy market town beside the
main road between Preston and Yorkshire, it had several
inns to serve its many visitors; the Swan and Royal was a
staging post for the mail coach. The building opposite is
the Conservative Club, which was built in 1929.

Clitheroe, Market Place c1950 C122003 More old pubs stand around the ancient market place. On the left are the Victoria Hotel and the White Lion, whilst the White Horse is a little further down. Overlooking the junction is the Carnegie Library, which opened in 1905, and behind is the Town Hall, built in 1820 on the site of the Moot Hall.

▼ **Chatburn, The Toll-House c1955** C462004

The building dividing the junction was built in 1739 as a toll-house, but since the late 1930s it has been the home of Hudson's ice cream. The secret recipe was devised by Margaret Hudson, daughter of the butcher who then owned the shop. Although it has since changed hands, the present owners continue to make the same delicious ice cream.

▼ **Downham, The Assheton Arms c1965** D16030

Once known as the George and Dragon, the village's pub changed its name to the Assheton Arms after Sir Ralph Cockayne Assheton was elevated to the peerage as Lord Clitheroe in 1945. The family have held the estate since 1558, and Downham's unspoilt beauty and unity owes much to their influence.

▲ **Downham, The Village c1965** D16023

Although the stream looks placid enough, it is prone to flooding: after a particularly severe inundation in 1962, the bridge was altered to ease the water flow. If you visit today, you will see no television aerials on the roofs, for Lord Clitheroe installed an underground cabled system to each house to preserve the unspoilt character of the village.

◄ **Roughlee, The Lake c1955**
R321002
Roughlee Lake was once a popular local day out. The lake, originally the reservoir for the cotton mill at the far end, was used for boating and swimming, whilst sunbathers and picnickers enjoyed its wooded banks. Below the lake, a small menagerie, pony rides and swingboats provided other entertainments. After closing in the 1970s, the lake is now a trout fishery.

Newchurch in Pendle, The Village c1955 N191001
Originally Goldshaw Booth, this small village is overlooked by Pendle Hill. Its present name derives from the rebuilding of St Mary's Church in 1740, but locals call it 't'Kirk'. An 18th-century handloom weaver's cottage houses the souvenir shop, where you can find out everything you want to know, and perhaps more, about the ancient witches of Pendle.

Sabden, Old Bull Bridge c1955 S691007
The bridge carries the Padiham road over Sabden Brook into the village. Thought to have been used since the Bronze Age, the track through the valley was one of several routes followed by packhorse drivers, who carried goods across the moorland hills between Lancashire and Yorkshire. Many inns, like the White Hart (centre), originated to serve the passing trade.

The Fylde and its Fringes

Wrea Green
The Green c1965 W527024
The life of the village is centred on this vast expanse of green.
Pictured here is the school, which was built in 1893, and beside
it, the Grapes Hotel. Not seen, just to the right, is the
19th-century church of St Nicholas. Around the other sides stand
attractive cottages, some of which are thatched.

Lytham, The Square
c1950 L128002
Many of Lytham's buildings date from its redevelopment as a select residential town and resort. Elaborate arcades front the shops, and an impressive cupola crowns the bank. Around the corner in Market Square stands the Market Hall, which was built in 1846, and close by is the estate office of the Cliftons, who owned the land on which Lytham grew.

Lytham
The Promenade and the Greens c1955 L128042
The wide green and promenade overlooking the Ribble estuary
provided a fine grandstand from which to watch ships passing along
the river to and from the great port of Preston. The windmill was built
in 1805, and continued to grind corn until damaged by fire in 1918.
Next to it stands the old lifeboat house, which is now a museum.

Ansdell, Woodlands Road c1955 A89013
Many Victorian banks were built on prestigious corner sites and were grand affairs, often, like this one, capped with a dome or cupola. Beyond, the street rises to the station past large houses accommodating ground floor shops. The town took its name from the Victorian artist Richard Ansdell RA, who built a summerhouse here in the 1860s.

St Anne's, The Square c1955 S3055
Extravagant Victorian buildings front a grand boulevard; it is so wide that it has room for hedged flower beds along its length. The town has recovered its air of prosperity after the hardships and shortages of the war years, and its growing affluence is demonstrated by the number of cars parked beside the pavements.

Fairhaven, Clifton Drive c1955 F2015
Comfortable houses and spacious gardens fronting wide, straight streets characterise the planned 19th-century development of the area. Trams used to run along Clifton Drive, and the kiosk on the right was a shelter for waiting passengers. The White Church, identified by its striking tower, was built from white-glazed bricks for the Congregationalists in 1912.

Fairhaven, The Bowling Green c1955 F2011
Bowls has long been a popular game in Lancashire, and there is considerable rivalry between the many clubs of its towns, villages and pubs. Known from the 13th century, bowling passed into history with the tradition that Sir Frances Drake played the game at Plymouth Hoe whilst watching the approach of the Spanish Armada.

Blackpool
The Central Promenade c1955 B116017
Beyond the tower, the North Pier, built in 1863, was the first of
three to be erected. Other attractions soon followed: the Winter
Gardens opened in 1878, and electric trams appeared along the
sea front in 1885. The tower, almost 520 feet high, took over three
years to construct and was modelled on Eiffel's tower in Paris.

**Blackpool
The Promenade
c1955** B116015
The coming of the
railway during the
middle of the 19th
century was the catalyst
that sparked
Blackpool's
development as a
holiday resort, and
factory and mill
workers flocked from
the northern industrial
towns. Such were their
numbers that the
tradition of 'wakes
weeks' was established,
ensuring that the town
could accommodate
the thousands of visitors
that arrived each
summer.

◄ **Bispham, The Palm Court c1955** B744001
Bispham lies just a little to the north of Blackpool's bright lights and seemingly non-stop amusements, and its sea-front hotels and guesthouses attracted holidaymakers seeking a more relaxing break away from it all. The Palm Court Hotel, which stands next door to the former Miner's Convalescent Home, was run as a Methodist holiday home.

◄ Blackpool, North Shore c1955
B116014

The promenade was begun in 1907. It includes the delightful linear garden we see here, which is slightly sunken to provide protection from the sometimes-bracing wind. The end of the summer season is celebrated by illuminations decorating six miles of sea front. Billed as the 'greatest free show on earth', the event began in 1912 with just eight arc lamps lighting up the promenade.

▼ Fleetwood
The Miniature Golf Course and Railway c1960   F33021

At a time when railway engineers were convinced of the impossibility of constructing a rail link over Shap, Fleetwood was conceived in the 1830s to link trains from London with steamers to Glasgow and Ireland. Although the west-coast railway was eventually built, taking with it the Scottish traffic, the town developed a busy fishing fleet and Irish trade and emerged as a popular holiday resort.

◄ Fleetwood
The Esplanade c1960
F33023

The view beyond the promenade is across the Wyre to Knott End-on-Sea, the short pier serving as the landing stage for the passenger ferry across the estuary. Clustered around its head hoardings advertise amusement arcades and gift shops. The cranes stand at the edge of Fleetwood's docks, which lie along the western bank of the river.

◀ **Newton, Newton Hall Holiday Park, the Camp Shop c1960**
N215023
A useful facility, the shop appears to stock just about everything a holidaymaker could ever want. At one time, the camp, which opened in 1948, was the only local place holding a music licence for Sunday evenings, and people used to come from Blackpool for the dances held in its club.

◄ Fleetwood, The Lighthouse and the Esplanade c1960

F33028

The lighthouse is one of two that were built in 1840 to mark a safe passage into Fleetwood's harbour. This one on the sea front is 30 feet high, and approaching ships set a course lining it with the second light, which lies just inland. The latter was modelled on the Pharos lighthouse in Alexandria and stands 60 feet taller.

▼ Staining, Thornfield Holiday Camp c1960 S694002

Thornfield has been a holiday site since the beginning of the 20th century, when accommodation was provided in wooden chalets. During the war it was requisitioned to house travelling people, whose nomadic lifestyle was prevented by wartime restrictions. The photograph shows the present owner's mother (on the right) standing outside the camp shop.

◄ Poulton-le-Fylde The Square c1955

P105005

Lining the centre of the street are the town's stocks, market cross, fish slab and whipping post; the lamp behind was erected to commemorate Queen Victoria's golden jubilee. At the back rises the 17th-century tower of St Chad's Church. Its interior was remodelled during the Georgian period, and contains an upper gallery, unusually running around three sides.

▼ **Hambleton, The Creek c1960** H452016
Here at Wardley's Creek, a crew waits patiently as the rising tide approaches its peak to float their yacht from its resting-place, cut from the muddy banks of the inlet. Local stories tell that smugglers once favoured these quiet haunts, and slipped in under the cover of darkness to land their illicit cargoes.

▼ **Hambleton, Shard Toll Bridge c1960** H452003
Although the River Wyre is here quite wide, it could be forded at low water, and Shard derives from a dialect word meaning 'cattle crossing'. Later, a ferry provided a safer passage, which operated until this toll bridge was built in 1864. It too has since been replaced by a modern road bridge that opened in 1993.

▲ **Knott End-on-Sea The Ferry and the Slipway c1950** K128006
Taken from the end of the promenade by the Bourne Arms, the scene shows the once-busy steam ferry arriving from Fleetwood across the Wyre estuary. On the far bank, to the left, lie Fleetwood's docks. The large building is the North Euston Hotel, and to its right is the lower of Fleetwood's two lighthouses.

◄ **Knott End-on-Sea Wyre View c1950** K128010
Although called Wyre View, the outlook is across Morecambe Bay to the Lake District. The distant backdrop is of the high fells, and on a clear day, it is possible to see England's highest mountains from the foreshore esplanade. A viewing table has now been positioned at the end of the street to help identify the far-off peaks.

▼ Preesall, The Village c1955 P344003

Occupying a hill-top, Preesall grew as a small market around a corn mill and two pubs, both of which are shown here, the Black Bull and the Saracen's Head. The village developed further after salt was discovered in 1872, and several wells were sunk to pump brine. However, the industry declined in the 1920s, after significant subsidence began to occur.

▼ Pilling, The Old Mill c1960 P270006

The Fylde plain once had many such mills, benefiting from the strong prevailing winds blowing unchecked off the Irish Sea. This one, standing 63 feet high, was built in 1808 and continued to grind corn until 1926, having been converted to steam in 1886. The mound in front of it marks a kiln that was used to dry the grain.

▲ Garstang, High Street c1955 G238007

Just beyond the Market House stands the Town Hall, its prominent clock tower topped by an intricate weather vane. Opened in 1755, it is the third such building to occupy the site - both its predecessors were destroyed by fire. Beyond is the Royal Oak Hotel, one of several old coaching inns that still stand in the town.

◄ **Garstang, Market Place c1965** G238046
The town's reputation for its fine market harks back to the 14th century, when the first rights were granted to the abbot of Cockersands. The stone pillar topped with an orb marks the site of the original cross and stands on a medieval base. The present column was erected in 1754 and was renovated in 1897 to mark Victoria's diamond jubilee.

▼ Garstang, Church Street c1955 G238016

Church Street leads from the Market Square down to the Lancaster Canal, where a basin facilitated the handling of cargo on and off the barges. Beyond the trees lies St Thomas' Church, where in 1997 a painting hanging on its walls, 'Ecce Homo', was realised to be an original work by Annebella Carracci; it was subsequently valued at £5 million.

▼ Garstang, The Six Arches c1960 G238063

Built around 1840 to carry the London and North Western railway line north through Lancashire, this splendid six-arch bridge strides across the River Wyre just below Scorton Lakes. From Victoria View, the backdrop to the scene is of the Lancashire fells, with the land rising to the summit of Calder Fell at its high spot.

▲ Churchtown
The Punch Bowl Inn
c1955 C603003

The Punch Bowl Inn was formerly known as the Covered Cup, a reference to the three chalices contained within the emblem of the Butler family, who held the manor. St Helen's Church, from where this photograph was taken, aptly deserves its epithet 'Cathedral of the Fylde': it is a magnificent building whose earliest parts date from the 12th century.

◀ **Little Eccleston, Cartford Lane c1965** G25070
A small caravan site and the Cartford Hotel flank the approach to the Cartford toll bridge, which was built across the Wyre in 1831. As implied by its name, there was originally a ford here, and it was one of the few places on the Fylde plain where the river could safely be crossed.

Inskip, The Cheese Factory c1950 164002
The lush Fylde pastures are particularly suited to dairy farming. At the Garstang Creamery, the area's rich milk was converted into cheese. However, economies of production and increasing regulation have brought the demise of many smaller cheese manufacturers; this factory has closed, and its site is now occupied by a small residential development.

Bilsborrow, The Roebuck Hotel c1960 B743006
Roebucks are the males of the roe deer, whose herds once roamed this attractive landscape along the western fringe of the Lancashire hills. Sited beside the main north road, the pub has always been a busy place, with the canal and, later, the railway also bringing their trade. The former nearby station took the name of Roebuck.

Bilsborrow
The Roebuck Hotel c1960 B743007
For both holidaymakers enjoying a coach excursion from
Blackpool and trippers travelling home after a day at the resort, the
Roebuck was a popular place to break the journey. Besides the
refreshments on offer, there was an opportunity for a stroll beside
the canal or, perhaps, a game of bowls on the pub's fine green.

◄ **Lancaster, Market Street c1950** L10038
On the corner of King Street is the King's Arms, where Charles Dickens stayed in 1857 and 1862. Towards the far end is the Old Town Hall, built in 1783 with an adorning cupola being added later. The ground floor arcading was originally open, and the building was used as the corn exchange; it now houses the city museum.

Around Lancaster
and the Lune Valley

◄ **Lancaster, John o' Gaunt's Statue
Main Gateway, Castle c1950** L10028
Prehistoric flints found here suggest that Castle Hill is an ancient defensive site. Roger Poitou began the present castle in 1093, and the gateway was added in the 1400s by John o' Gaunt's son, who had seized the throne in 1399 to become Henry IV. From that time on, the Crown has held the Duchy of Lancaster.

◄ **Lancaster, Market Street c1950** L10042
The façade of the Old Town Hall is here more evident, and the pub on the right remembers Lancaster's associations with John o'Gaunt. A ginnel on the left, Sun Street, leads to the elegant 18th-century Music Room. Thought to have been built as a garden summerhouse and now restored by the Landmark Trust, its plaster decoration depicts the Muses.

◄ **Cockerham**
The Manor Inn c1955
C599008
Originally clustered around the church to the south, the hamlet was destroyed by a fire in the 17th century and the Manor Inn, built in 1871, is the focus of the 'new' village. Although quiet-looking here, the village was known for its boisterous sporting events, with such things as cock fights, greyhound coursing and horseracing being organised.

Dolphinholme Church Corner c1955
D210003

These 18th-century stone cottages were built for workers at the nearby mill, which was originally water-driven - its wheel was second only in size to that of Laxey on the Isle of Man. In 1811, the village and factory were amongst the first to be lit by gas, and in 1822 the mill was converted to steam.

Galgate, The Village c1960 G284004

Pictured from Highland Brow, the scene looks across the railway and the A6 to Thompson Mill, which operated as a silk mill from 1792 until 1971. Originally a water-powered corn-mill, it was converted to steam and considerably extended during the 19th century. The cottages of the village are shown to the right.

Galgate The Post Office c1960
G284019

The post office, the Green Dragon and, opposite, the New Inn, overlook the cross-roads at the centre of the village. Galgate's inns once played a part in nominating the village 'mayor'. The annual fair was inevitably accompanied by excessive drinking, and the first man found sleeping it off in the hedgerows the following morning was given the honour.

▼ Glasson Dock, Victoria Terrace c1955 G260011

The Caribou Hotel overlooks the basin and locks, which connect the Lancaster Branch Canal with the sea. Glasson was first used as a port for ships unable to navigate the Lune to Lancaster from 1787, but the arrival of the canal in 1826, followed by the railway in 1883, increased its effectiveness.

▼ Hest Bank, Marine Drive c1960 H453015

If we turn left at the junction and cross the railway line, we find ourselves on the shore, from where stagecoaches began their dangerous crossing of the bay to Lonsdale North of the Sands. Before the railway arrived, the overland journey involved a lengthy detour around the head of the estuary, but many lost their lives in attempting this more direct route.

▲ Bare, The Promenade c1955 B741001

To the north of Morecambe is the quieter sea front of Bare. The promenade guesthouses and private hotels enjoy superb views across the bay to Lancashire over Sands and the southern Lake District. Once little more than a fishing village, the area became popular as a sea-bathing resort during the mid 19th century after the arrival of the railway.

◄ **Torrisholme
A Waggonette
at the George Hotel
c1965** T238026A
A favourite treat for
holidaymakers to
Morecambe was a trip on
one of these horse-drawn
buses, which left the
promenade for a short
excursion out of town. A
favourite stopping place
was the George Hotel at
Torrisholme, where the
passengers could enjoy a
drink, whilst the horses
were no doubt grateful for
a brief rest.

Morecambe Central Beach c1955

M94022

Morecambe, popular with day-trippers and holidaymakers, boasted several large hotels along its sea front. At the far end is the Midland, and carrying an advertisement for the Palladium Cinema is the Crown. Opposite the Kings Arms a lively statue has now been placed as a tribute to the much-loved comedian Eric Morecambe, who took his hometown for his stage name.

▼ Heysham, Half Moon Bay c1960 H81042

Away from the bright lights and entertainments of its main resorts, Lancashire's coast has many other fine stretches of expansive beach. Half Moon Bay, which lies north of Heysham Docks, was a popular destination for a day on the sands. Children paddle in the shallow waters or investigate the rock pools, whilst others dig castles from the soft sand.

▼ Lower Heysham, Main Street c1965 L474050

Growing from a small fishing village to an unpretentious resort during the middle of the 19th century, Lower Heysham has retained its 'olde world' atmosphere. Many of its cottages were built in the 17th century, and the Royal Oak is older, claiming a date of about 1502. A famous treat, which is still sold today, was Granny's Nettle Beer.

▲ Lower Heysham Main Street c1955

L474006

Some of the visitors who enjoyed a stroll through the village streets came from the nearby Morecambe Bay Holiday Camp. Set in Heysham Towers, which was formerly the home of the Knowles family, it was open from 1925 until 1972, except for a period during the war years when it was conscripted by the military.

◄ **Lower Heysham
The Entrance to Heysham
Head c1965** L474054
Septimus Wray opened the
estate on Heysham Head as
an amusement park in
1926. Apart from gardens
and woodland walks, the
various entertainments
included a bandstand, a
dancing bear, marionette
shows and a zoo. The
complex was taken over by
the Council in the 1970s,
but its heyday had passed
and it finally closed in
1983.

◀ **Halton**
The View from Castle Hill
c1955 H506008
The Romans were the first to exploit the defensive qualities of this hill; later strongholds were erected during the Saxon era and in the 11th century. Below is St Wilfrid's, founded in the 7th century, and rebuilt many times since. It contains a number of 9th-century crosses, and above the porch is a half-timbered room.

◄ Lower Heysham
The Cliff Walk c1955 L474008
The low coastal cliffs below the village provided a pleasant walk above the beach. Hidden by the trees is St Peter's Church, believed to have been founded in 967. Behind that stands a ruined chapel, perhaps two centuries older, and below it are eight remarkable shallow graves cut into the headland rock, possibly the tombs of priests or chiefs.

▼ Caton, Brookhouse c1960
C473038
St Paul's Church, behind the cottages, was founded in the 13th century. Rebuilt by the Tudors and again by the Victorians, it contains interesting relics of its history. Re-set in the bridge opposite the Black Bull Inn, by which the photographer stood, is a hollow plague stone where villagers left money to pay for their goods.

◄ Caton, Penny Bridge
c1960 C473054
Well before it became a favourite bathing and picnic spot, the Lune's beauties at Caton were extolled by the poets Wordsworth and Gray, and Turner came to paint the scene. The first bridge was built in 1806, but it collapsed in 1881 and travellers had to resort to the original ford until the present structure was opened two years later.

▼ Hornby, The War Memorial c 1965 H454026

Beside the main road through the village on the base of the ancient cross is an elaborate war memorial. It stands outside St Mary's Catholic Church, which was built by John Lingard, who came to the village in 1811. A priest and historian, amongst his many works was a much-acclaimed eight-volume 'History of England'.

▼ Hornby, The Castle Hotel c1965 H454028

Pictured from outside Hornby's Anglican church is the Castle Hotel. During the 18th century, the village was a halt for stage coaches travelling between Lancaster and Kirkby Lonsdale. Passengers occupying the roof seats were able to enter the hotel directly through an upper door, saving them the nuisance of having to clamber down from the coach.

▲ Wray, The Village c1950

W588003

Viewed from above the River Roeburn, the scene overlooks the roofs of the village cottages, most of which were put up during the 17th and 18th centuries. There were a number of mills here. They took their power from the Roeburn and Hindburn, and served several industries that included nail-making, hatting, wood-turning and sawing.

◄ **Bolton-le-Sands**
The Village c1960 B137022
Bolton-le-Sands is perched on a low rise that once overlooked the sea. Its former maritime associations are reflected in the name of the Blue Anchor. Behind it stands the square 15th-century embattled tower of Holy Trinity Church. Previously dedicated to St Michael, the church has an ancient history; it incorporates stones from a pre-Norman building.

▼ **Bolton-le-Sands, The Nook c1960** B137032
Taken from outside St Mary of the Angels, the village's Catholic church, this view looks along The Nook past 17th- and early 18th-century houses. Many of the cottages carry date stones with the initials of the families that built them over their doorways. Notice too, the prominent dripstones incorporated above window and door openings.

▼ **Over Kellet, The Green c1960** O88003
Quartered by a cross-roads, the spacious green contains two monuments. The nearer is a war memorial and the other is a massive stone cross, erected on the base of the original village cross. It is said that in the 7th century St Cuthbert passed through the settlement, an event remembered in the dedication of the village's church.

▲ **Carnforth, Lancaster Road c1955** C35004
Carnforth's industries of sand and gravel extraction and iron smelting depended upon the Lancaster Canal and later the railway, when an important junction between the north-south and east-west lines was created here. The station, which lies a short distance to the left along Market Street, was used as a set during the filming of 'Brief Encounter'.

◀ Warton, Main Street and the Church c1955

W30005

The Washington family (a descendent became the first president of America), funded the construction of the tower to St Oswald's Church. The village maintains a strong connection with the USA: the Stars and Stripes are flown from the top of the tower on Independence Day, and the Black Bull Hotel has been renamed the George Washington.

Yealand Conyers, The Village c1955 Y7018
An assortment of attractive cottages lines the quiet street, and behind the wall on the left is the village pump. The place has strong connections with the Quaker movement, and George Fox visited in 1652. Close by is a Friends' Meeting House and burial ground, said to be the oldest in the country, which was built in 1692.

Yealand Redmayne, Cottages, Main Street c1955 Y48009
Lying at the foot of wooded limestone slopes to the east of Cringlebarrow, these rendered stone cottages, with pronounced dripstones protecting their windows and doorways from the rain, are typical of the vernacular style. Many of them were built during the late 17th and 18th centuries.

Silverdale
Emesgate Lane c1955 S609011
Now a relative backwater, Silverdale was an embarkation point for the
hazardous trip across the sands to Grange. It was also a small port, but
the ever-changing course of the River Kent has left it without sufficient
draught. However, the place is still busy with visitors, and the Royal
Hotel continues its tradition of hospitality that began before the 1890s.

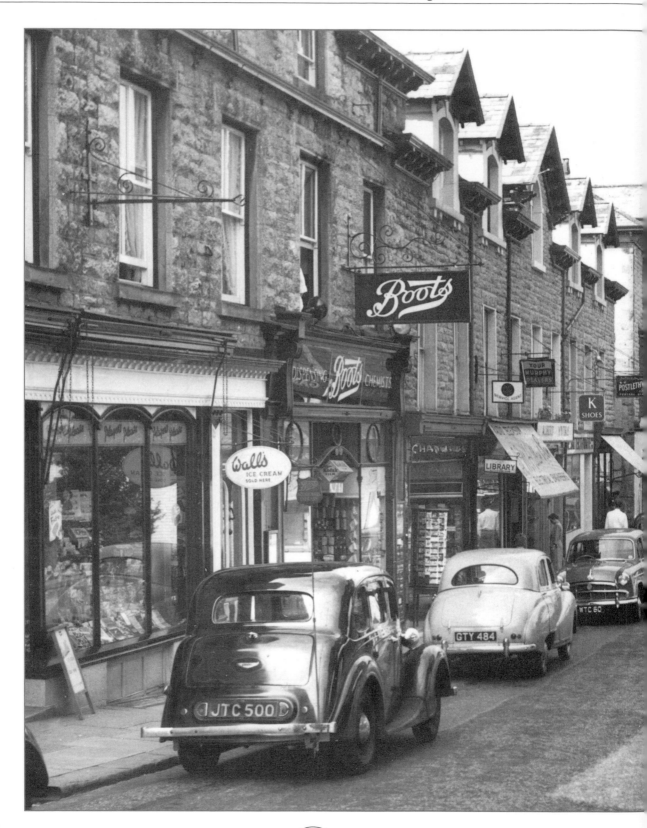

Furness

Grange-over-Sands, Main Street c1955 G42087
Much of Grange was constructed during the later
19th century from local stone and slate, and there
is a pleasing uniformity to the buildings that line its
principal shopping street. Higher up Main Street
stands the Grange Institute, a social and recreation
centre and the base for the town's snooker club,
where there are two fine slate snooker tables.

◀ **Cartmel, The View across the Village c1955** C40047
Seen from below Fell End towards Howbarrow and Mount Barnard, the priory church of St Mary and St Michael stands prominently at the centre of the village. Behind, to the left, is the famous Cartmel Race Course. Tradition has it that the races were begun by the monks as an entertainment to celebrate Whitsuntide.

Grange-over-Sands The Ornamental Gardens c1955 G42077

The gardens, which lie beside the railway station, were opened in 1865. Attractive flower beds and shrubberies surround an ornamental lake, which draws large numbers of water birds. Overlooking the water, the town's war memorial, styled as a 7th-century Celtic cross, was designed by the Lancaster architects Austin and Paley, whose work appears in many of the area's churches.

Cartmel, The Square c1955 C40008

At the centre of the village is the ancient market cross and priory gatehouse, now owned by the National Trust. Although first founded in the 7th century by St Cuthbert, the present priory church and ruins relate to a later Augustinian community established in about 1190. It was largely destroyed after the Dissolution, but the magnificent church and gatehouse have survived.

Ulverston, The Cross c1950 U5008

Ulverston evolved as a market town for the surrounding farms and villages, and required many cafes and inns to meet the demands for refreshment on market day. The photograph was taken from the Sun Inn and looks across to three other pubs. Behind the war memorial is a seed and agricultural merchant, an important store in a rural town.

Ulverston, King Street 1950 U5028
This view along the main street towards the Market Square displays an air of rural pragmatism, with several of the shops displaying their wares for inspection outside. In 1890, the town was the birthplace of Arthur Stanley Jefferson, better known as Stan Laurel, and a museum in Upper Brook Street, off to the right, celebrates his partnership with Oliver Hardy.

Coniston
Tarn Hows c1960 C153046
Tarn Hows is deservedly one of the
most renowned beauty spots in
Lakeland, a meandering lake set in a
wooded hollow with a backdrop of
rugged mountains gracing the skyline.
Surprisingly, however, the view is totally
man-made, for the lake was created as
a reservoir to power a sawmill and
much of the woodland was planted as
a cash crop.

Hawkshead
The Pillar House c1955 H47002
These cottages are typical of this lovely
Lakeland village, which clusters
around its 16th-century church. The
poet William Wordsworth and his
brother Richard attended the grammar
school here, and Beatrix Potter
married the local solicitor, William
Heelis. His former office, now in the
care of the National Trust, is opened
as a gallery, displaying illustrations
from her children's books.

Index

Frith Book Co Titles

www.francisfrith.co.uk

The Frith Book Company publishes over 100 new titles each year. A selection of those currently available are listed below. For latest catalogue please contact Frith Book Co.

Town Books 96 pages, approx 100 photos. County and Themed Books 128 pages, approx 150 photos (unless specified). All titles hardback laminated case and jacket except those indicated pb (paperback)

Title	ISBN	Price	Title	ISBN	Price
Amersham, Chesham & Rickmansworth (pb)	1-85937-340-2	£9.99	Derby (pb)	1-85937-367-4	£9.99
Ancient Monuments & Stone Circles	1-85937-143-4	£17.99	Derbyshire (pb)	1-85937-196-5	£9.99
Aylesbury (pb)	1-85937-227-9	£9.99	Devon (pb)	1-85937-297-x	£9.99
Bakewell	1-85937-113-2	£12.99	Dorset (pb)	1-85937-269-4	£9.99
Barnstaple (pb)	1-85937-300-3	£9.99	Dorset Churches	1-85937-172-8	£17.99
Bath (pb)	1-85937419-0	£9.99	Dorset Coast (pb)	1-85937-299-6	£9.99
Bedford (pb)	1-85937-205-8	£9.99	Dorset Living Memories	1-85937-210-4	£14.99
Berkshire (pb)	1-85937-191-4	£9.99	Down the Severn	1-85937-118-3	£14.99
Berkshire Churches	1-85937-170-1	£17.99	Down the Thames (pb)	1-85937-278-3	£9.99
Blackpool (pb)	1-85937-382-8	£9.99	Down the Trent	1-85937-311-9	£14.99
Bognor Regis (pb)	1-85937-431-x	£9.99	Dublin (pb)	1-85937-231-7	£9.99
Bournemouth	1-85937-067-5	£12.99	East Anglia (pb)	1-85937-265-1	£9.99
Bradford (pb)	1-85937-204-x	£9.99	East London	1-85937-080-2	£14.99
Brighton & Hove(pb)	1-85937-192-2	£8.99	East Sussex	1-85937-130-2	£14.99
Bristol (pb)	1-85937-264-3	£9.99	Eastbourne	1-85937-061-6	£12.99
British Life A Century Ago (pb)	1-85937-213-9	£9.99	Edinburgh (pb)	1-85937-193-0	£8.99
Buckinghamshire (pb)	1-85937-200-7	£9.99	England in the 1880s	1-85937-331-3	£17.99
Camberley (pb)	1-85937-222-8	£9.99	English Castles (pb)	1-85937-434-4	£9.99
Cambridge (pb)	1-85937-422-0	£9.99	English Country Houses	1-85937-161-2	£17.99
Cambridgeshire (pb)	1-85937-420-4	£9.99	Essex (pb)	1-85937-270-8	£9.99
Canals & Waterways (pb)	1-85937-291-0	£9.99	Exeter	1-85937-126-4	£12.99
Canterbury Cathedral (pb)	1-85937-179-5	£9.99	Exmoor	1-85937-132-9	£14.99
Cardiff (pb)	1-85937-093-4	£9.99	Falmouth	1-85937-066-7	£12.99
Carmarthenshire	1-85937-216-3	£14.99	Folkestone (pb)	1-85937-124-8	£9.99
Chelmsford (pb)	1-85937-310-0	£9.99	Glasgow (pb)	1-85937-190-6	£9.99
Cheltenham (pb)	1-85937-095-0	£9.99	Gloucestershire	1-85937-102-7	£14.99
Cheshire (pb)	1-85937-271-6	£9.99	Great Yarmouth (pb)	1-85937-426-3	£9.99
Chester	1-85937-090-x	£12.99	Greater Manchester (pb)	1-85937-266-x	£9.99
Chesterfield	1-85937-378-x	£9.99	Guildford (pb)	1-85937-410-7	£9.99
Chichester (pb)	1-85937-228-7	£9.99	Hampshire (pb)	1-85937-279-1	£9.99
Colchester (pb)	1-85937-188-4	£8.99	Hampshire Churches (pb)	1-85937-207-4	£9.99
Cornish Coast	1-85937-163-9	£14.99	Harrogate	1-85937-423-9	£9.99
Cornwall (pb)	1-85937-229-5	£9.99	Hastings & Bexhill (pb)	1-85937-131-0	£9.99
Cornwall Living Memories	1-85937-248-1	£14.99	Heart of Lancashire (pb)	1-85937-197-3	£9.99
Cotswolds (pb)	1-85937-230-9	£9.99	Helston (pb)	1-85937-214-7	£9.99
Cotswolds Living Memories	1-85937-255-4	£14.99	Hereford (pb)	1-85937-175-2	£9.99
County Durham	1-85937-123-x	£14.99	Herefordshire	1-85937-174-4	£14.99
Croydon Living Memories	1-85937-162-0	£9.99	Hertfordshire (pb)	1-85937-247-3	£9.99
Cumbria	1-85937-101-9	£14.99	Horsham (pb)	1-85937-432-8	£9.99
Dartmoor	1-85937-145-0	£14.99	Humberside	1-85937-215-5	£14.99
			Hythe, Romney Marsh & Ashford	1-85937-256-2	£9.99

Available from your local bookshop or from the publisher

Frith Book Co Titles (continued)

Title	ISBN	Price	Title	ISBN	Price
Ipswich (pb)	1-85937-424-7	£9.99	St Ives (pb)	1-85937415-8	£9.99
Ireland (pb)	1-85937-181-7	£9.99	Scotland (pb)	1-85937-182-5	£9.99
Isle of Man (pb)	1-85937-268-6	£9.99	Scottish Castles (pb)	1-85937-323-2	£9.99
Isles of Scilly	1-85937-136-1	£14.99	Sevenoaks & Tunbridge	1-85937-057-8	£12.99
Isle of Wight (pb)	1-85937-429-8	£9.99	Sheffield, South Yorks (pb)	1-85937-267-8	£9.99
Isle of Wight Living Memories	1-85937-304-6	£14.99	Shrewsbury (pb)	1-85937-325-9	£9.99
Kent (pb)	1-85937-189-2	£9.99	Shropshire (pb)	1-85937-326-7	£9.99
Kent Living Memories	1-85937-125-6	£14.99	Somerset	1-85937-153-1	£14.99
Lake District (pb)	1-85937-275-9	£9.99	South Devon Coast	1-85937-107-8	£14.99
Lancaster, Morecambe & Heysham (pb)	1-85937-233-3	£9.99	South Devon Living Memories	1-85937-168-x	£14.99
Leeds (pb)	1-85937-202-3	£9.99	South Hams	1-85937-220-1	£14.99
Leicester	1-85937-073-x	£12.99	Southampton (pb)	1-85937-427-1	£9.99
Leicestershire (pb)	1-85937-185-x	£9.99	Southport (pb)	1-85937-425-5	£9.99
Lincolnshire (pb)	1-85937-433-6	£9.99	Staffordshire	1-85937-047-0	£12.99
Liverpool & Merseyside (pb)	1-85937-234-1	£9.99	Stratford upon Avon	1-85937-098-5	£12.99
London (pb)	1-85937-183-3	£9.99	Suffolk (pb)	1-85937-221-x	£9.99
Ludlow (pb)	1-85937-176-0	£9.99	Suffolk Coast	1-85937-259-7	£14.99
Luton (pb)	1-85937-235-x	£9.99	Surrey (pb)	1-85937-240-6	£9.99
Maidstone	1-85937-056-x	£14.99	Sussex (pb)	1-85937-184-1	£9.99
Manchester (pb)	1-85937-198-1	£9.99	Swansea (pb)	1-85937-167-1	£9.99
Middlesex	1-85937-158-2	£14.99	Tees Valley & Cleveland	1-85937-211-2	£14.99
New Forest	1-85937-128-0	£14.99	Thanet (pb)	1-85937-116-7	£9.99
Newark (pb)	1-85937-366-6	£9.99	Tiverton (pb)	1-85937-178-7	£9.99
Newport, Wales (pb)	1-85937-258-9	£9.99	Torbay	1-85937-063-2	£12.99
Newquay (pb)	1-85937-421-2	£9.99	Truro	1-85937-147-7	£12.99
Norfolk (pb)	1-85937-195-7	£9.99	Victorian and Edwardian Cornwall	1-85937-252-x	£14.99
Norfolk Living Memories	1-85937-217-1	£14.99	Victorian & Edwardian Devon	1-85937-253-8	£14.99
Northamptonshire	1-85937-150-7	£14.99	Victorian & Edwardian Kent	1-85937-149-3	£14.99
Northumberland Tyne & Wear (pb)	1-85937-281-3	£9.99	Vic & Ed Maritime Album	1-85937-144-2	£17.99
North Devon Coast	1-85937-146-9	£14.99	Victorian and Edwardian Sussex	1-85937-157-4	£14.99
North Devon Living Memories	1-85937-261-9	£14.99	Victorian & Edwardian Yorkshire	1-85937-154-x	£14.99
North London	1-85937-206-6	£14.99	Victorian Seaside	1-85937-159-0	£17.99
North Wales (pb)	1-85937-290-8	£9.99	Villages of Devon (pb)	1-85937-293-7	£9.99
North Yorkshire (pb)	1-85937-236-8	£9.99	Villages of Kent (pb)	1-85937-294-5	£9.99
Norwich (pb)	1-85937-194-9	£8.99	Villages of Sussex (pb)	1-85937-295-3	£9.99
Nottingham (pb)	1-85937-324-0	£9.99	Warwickshire (pb)	1-85937-203-1	£9.99
Nottinghamshire (pb)	1-85937-187-6	£9.99	Welsh Castles (pb)	1-85937-322-4	£9.99
Oxford (pb)	1-85937-411-5	£9.99	West Midlands (pb)	1-85937-289-9	£9.99
Oxfordshire (pb)	1-85937-430-1	£9.99	West Sussex	1-85937-148-5	£14.99
Peak District (pb)	1-85937-280-5	£9.99	West Yorkshire (pb)	1-85937-201-5	£9.99
Penzance	1-85937-069-1	£12.99	Weymouth (pb)	1-85937-209-0	£9.99
Peterborough (pb)	1-85937-219-8	£9.99	Wiltshire (pb)	1-85937-277-5	£9.99
Piers	1-85937-237-6	£17.99	Wiltshire Churches (pb)	1-85937-171-x	£9.99
Plymouth	1-85937-119-1	£12.99	Wiltshire Living Memories	1-85937-245-7	£14.99
Poole & Sandbanks (pb)	1-85937-251-1	£9.99	Winchester (pb)	1-85937-428-x	£9.99
Preston (pb)	1-85937-212-0	£9.99	Windmills & Watermills	1-85937-242-2	£17.99
Reading (pb)	1-85937-238-4	£9.99	Worcester (pb)	1-85937-165-5	£9.99
Romford (pb)	1-85937-319-4	£9.99	Worcestershire	1-85937-152-3	£14.99
Salisbury (pb)	1-85937-239-2	£9.99	York (pb)	1-85937-199-x	£9.99
Scarborough (pb)	1-85937-379-8	£9.99	Yorkshire (pb)	1-85937-186-8	£9.99
St Albans (pb)	1-85937-341-0	£9.99	Yorkshire Living Memories	1-85937-166-3	£14.99

See Frith books on the internet www.francisfrith.co.uk

FRITH PRODUCTS & SERVICES

Francis Frith would doubtless be pleased to know that the pioneering publishing venture he started in 1860 still continues today. A hundred and forty years later, The Francis Frith Collection continues in the same innovative tradition and is now one of the foremost publishers of vintage photographs in the world. Some of the current activities include:

Interior Decoration

Today Frith's photographs can be seen framed and as giant wall murals in thousands of pubs, restaurants, hotels, banks, retail stores and other public buildings throughout the country. In every case they enhance the unique local atmosphere of the places they depict and provide reminders of gentler days in an increasingly busy and frenetic world.

Product Promotions

Frith products are used by many major companies to promote the sales of their own products or to reinforce their own history and heritage. Frith promotions have been used by Hovis bread, Courage beers, Scots Porage Oats, Colman's mustard, Cadbury's foods, Mellow Birds coffee, Dunhill pipe tobacco, Guinness, and Bulmer's Cider.

Genealogy and Family History

As the interest in family history and roots grows world-wide, more and more people are turning to Frith's photographs of Great Britain for images of the towns, villages and streets where their ancestors lived; and, of course, photographs of the churches and chapels where their ancestors were christened, married and buried are an essential part of every genealogy tree and family album.

Frith Products

All Frith photographs are available Framed or just as Mounted Prints and Posters (size 23 x 16 inches). These may be ordered from the address below. From time to time other products - Address Books, Calendars, Table Mats, etc - are available.

The Internet

Already twenty thousand Frith photographs can be viewed and purchased on the internet through the Frith websites and a myriad of partner sites.

For more detailed information on Frith companies and products, look at these sites:

www.francisfrith.co.uk
www.francisfrith.com
(for North American visitors)

See the complete list of Frith Books at:

www.francisfrith.co.uk

This web site is regularly updated with the latest list of publications from the Frith Book Company. If you wish to buy books relating to another part of the country that your local bookshop does not stock, you may purchase on-line.

For further information, trade, or author enquiries please contact us at the address below:
The Francis Frith Collection, Frith's Barn, Teffont, Salisbury, Wiltshire, England SP3 5QP.
Tel: +44 (0)1722 716 376 Fax: +44 (0)1722 716 881 Email: sales@francisfrith.co.uk

---

See Frith books on the internet www.francisfrith.co.uk